Blister Pack

DAVID McCOOEY was born in 1967 and has lived in Australia since
1970. He is the author of the prize-winning critical work, *Artful
Histories: Modern Australian Autobiography*. As well as a poet, he is one of
Australia's leading poetry critics. He is a senior lecturer in literary
studies at Deakin University and the associate editor of *Space: New
Writing*.

Blister Pack

DAVID MCCOOEY

CAMBRIDGE

PUBLISHED BY SALT PUBLISHING
PO Box 937, Great Wilbraham, Cambridge PDO CB1 5JX United Kingdom

© David McCooey, 2005

First published 2005

Printed and bound in the United Kingdom by Lightning Source

Typeset in Swift 9.5 / 13

ISBN 1 84471 052 1 paperback

Australian Government

Australia Council
for the Arts

*This project has been assisted by the Australian Government
through the Australia Council, its arts funding and advisory body.*

1 3 5 7 9 8 6 4 2

for Kate McCooey

Contents

Acknowledgments

Poems in this collection have previously appeared in *Australian Book Review*, *The Age*, *Antipodes* (USA), *core*, *Poetry Review* (UK), *poetryetc* (online), *Southerly*, *Verse* (USA), and *Westerly*.

Long overdue thanks are due to the following for their advice and encouragement: Kevin Brophy, Justin Clemens, Laurie Duggan, Kevin Hart, Dennis Haskell, Paul Kane, John Kinsella, Anthony Lynch, Noel Rowe, Vivian Smith, Chris Wallace-Crabbe.

Thank you to Maria Takolander: ideal reader.

Part I

Occupations

Well, I don't live in London, but I
Might have been born there. There's something
To be said for silence; the houses
In Bendigo and Geelong that don't
Have anyone living above or below them.
The quietude of the margins is
Quite an illumination; though
Trucks from one part of the country
Are always passing through to another.

And there's my friend in New York City
Who used to look a bit like John Lennon.
Why do all the clever people leave home?
They only have to find a home somewhere else.
And people in flats are always playing
Sondheim or Sinead O'Connor at thoughtless
Hours of the night. This is what the suburbs
Were invented for: never having to leave home;
Where artists can occupy a Belgium of the mind.

Questions in Philosophy
After Keats

Asking questions for a living,
It's easy to forget their name.

We might ask: what is a question?
Questions are not questions until

They are asked of our pulses
When they are faint, or halting,

When the world outside the window
Needn't ask what day it is, or

What pre-dates the predator?
Or what belies the believable?

French with Tears

pour Robin et Virginia

[1] RAISON D'ÊTRE

Music must change, but cafés stay the same.
Her hair remained in place even though
Her nose was out of joint. Well, that was
One way of putting it. You cannot see
Your reflection in the Yarra-coloured
Coffee, but you begin to muse upon
The narcissism of acquired taste,
How even democrats can be born to rule,
That the virtue of marriage is based on vice,
And those with time to muse on time are lost
Or young or old or sick. How briefly we
Fit none of those descriptions. You pay with
Change, which renders time's percussive music.

Three a.m. is the time for tragedies
Or parties (sometimes both). But when alone
It is a different kind of time, when Mind
Can glimpse its shadow, and entertain
Those moments of I-know-not-what: the sound
Of bells, or just after; the sight of clouds
Upon the milky page of childhood; the
Nostalgia of trains; and grappling with verbs.
And a moment, not for anything so
Unsubtle as revelation, but a
Stillness, of empty longing, homesickness
At home: echo of a question hitting
The walls of the well as it goes down, or
Else the mirror saying, 'I know not what.'

[3] NOBLESSE OBLIGE

They are always with us: in weekend houses,
Safe seats, high offices and cars. Vested
Interests, misrepresentation, even
Indifference: they have their obligations.
Perhaps there is a little voice asking
'Are you proud of your pride?' The question curls
Like smoke back into your eyes. You think:
'I am just a humble intellectual,
A simple man with complex dreams.' But there
Are thousands in high offices and cars,
All are humming to the obbligato
Of power, their minds as darkly lit as a
70s film, every one of their thoughts
As important as a supermodel.

|4| UNE BLESSURE

In the classroom it's all academic.
Books yawn upon the desks, eyes rest open.
In playgrounds boys will clutch their chests and say
'I'm hit,' or dream of walking with a limp.
Somewhere wars are being fought, or people
Being cut from broken cars. The hands
All taking notes in Physiology
Are steady, but do not think upon the
Future. All flesh is wounded by flesh, and
So is blessed as well. And in the classroom
You will look to see which clever student
Will know the link between 'to bless' and 'wound,'
And you will wonder if such things are learned
Or solely guessed within the bones, the breath.

[5] Plus ça change, plus c'est la même chose

Lionized MPs explain to us the more
We have the more we are, but when things change,
Inevitably we are shown the more
We lose the more we know. MPs? they stay
In marginal seats for life, while the same
Papers and private schools are showing more
Of the imaginary, expensive things
Your child will need for all our lives to change.
Teachers and journos may not care anymore
That courtly life won't offer us a stay
In proceedings: each sentence is the same.
They too just grow older the more things change.
Lions tame in the zoo the more they stay,
But our children hope for blood, just the same.

Dabbing eau de Cologne behind your ears,
While Roger limps to the *bureau de change*
(He manages things, he's so *dégagé*)
You think of well-known ways to spend the cash.
'*Les jeux sont faits*' rings in those scented ears;
Computers whirr like loaded roulette wheels;
Tourists from New York enumerate their rights:
Travel always is a *rite de passage.*
Roger returns *avec* a *New Yorker* —
Inside's a piece on *fin de siècle* —
Suggesting you to take him to Paris
('*Paris vaut bien une masse,*' so we're told).
À propos of nothing, some trivial
Thought comes to you in French, tongue of *ennui.*

[7] DÉJÀ VU

'I think that I have been through this before,'
Is all that you can think, for *déjà vu*
Will always sound both clichéd and contrived
If you should try to explicate its form.
In fact, it's formless and just another
Moment we are helpless to express.
How odd that things as singular as these
Should prove inimical to memory,
The way two minus signs will meet and turn
To zero, the way a galaxy in space
Is just a spray of light across the mind.
Why are anger and desire given
Anchors in the soul? . . . or is the soul
Extended *déjà vu* of angels?

[7] DÉJÀ VU

'I think that I have been through this before,'
But you can't fathom when. It comes to you
As if it lacked a source, like unseen storms
That send the wind to stagger through the streets.
As if the world's become too familiar
It breeds in unknown junctures: when you drive
Into a town that secretly has kept
Some part of childhood hostage; or strangers'
Conversation that's been lifted from a script,
Like living life inside an unwatched film.
Perhaps all lives are kept aside for
Other people's *déjà vu*. But moments
Such as these will pass, and in return leave
Ancient time's perpetual change, its music.

Signal-to-Noise Ratio

The refrigerator keeps in time with cool darkness.
A video records, though the screen is blank.
Even the stereo cannot be silent.
Its lines are open and are noisy.
It listens to itself and hums.

This is locking up at night, *fin de siècle.*
Who knows what real silence is?
Outside, the city is in second gear.
I close the door and wonder
At the inexhaustible self-expression of things.

Only the clock, like time, seems silent;
Its LED flicking over with infinite indifference,
As if dealing out a pack of jokers.
My pen is rasping out a name I almost know.
And you? Can you hear me listening to myself?

Evening

The cat, as black as a glassful of Guinness
Purrs like a stomach rumbling at morning.

The setting sun, golden as honey
Leaves the sting of another day wasted.

The empty bed, as restful as water
Tells of a flood from which I'll not wake.

    The cat and the sun at the foot of my bed
    Both greet me at dawn; another life left.

On Something

It's as if you're on something:
Drugs perhaps, but more likely
The world, a great big island

Floating in a sea of memory.
Your desert-island discs are
Stacked under the palms, but who

Needs music when you have the
Whispers of waves to put you
To sleep? The footprints by the

Shore could be yours or someone
Else's, but who can tell at
This hour of the day? A ship

Cruises by; you can hear a
Party on board. All of the
Passengers have got dressed up

To cross the equator. They're
Definitely on something
Which slips past you, but you don't

Care. This afternoon you're on
Fire, and for once your beacon
Doesn't spell out 'S.O.S.'

Circus Oz

Acts of mastery always involve suffering.
The upside down clown on the roof
   can't drink his whisky;
The galahs on the trapeze
   cannot fly a jot;
People fall from great heights
   or squeeze themselves
   into the tightest spaces.
The bicyclist's tyres are on fire.
We in the dark are left to consider
   the instructive effects
   of an excess of balance.

The Developed World

A plane flies over deserts. Listening to the
'Relaxation' channel we dream of caravans.

Below, photographers are taking pictures:
But we are photographed only by consent.

The paper swims in its tray, mildly enough.
But the images hanging up to dry are wrong:

Not quite in focus, something missing —
The sound of an aeroplane overhead, invisible.

Seen from a Train

A caravan ; some cars;
men working on the line;
while overhead the pale sky
softly unfolds
a slow dance of immense indirection.

Distance

Feeling safe inside my car
I watch the distance threaten rain,
And ignore a blur of gum trees

To my left. The radio tries
To drown the engine, fails, but the
Engine says nothing so is soon

Forgotten. Just outside Melbourne
I hear your name announced and then
Your voice appears, utterly

Unmagical, as everyday
As the speed limit. I drive
Towards the clouds, and your grainy

Voice in real time is listing the past:
Names, music, faraway childhood,
Destined for underground archives

Of tape. Your voice was everywhere,
And nowhere, until with the rain
Came the news, the traffic lights, a

Familiar junction, to which this
Day had been headed all along:
A town in the distance called home.

Melbourne Cup Day

Outside the birds cry,
indifferent to the tears
of the winners and losers

an hour's drive away.
The trees rustle their leaves
as punters finger their

betting slips. Somebody
turns on the radio and
the afternoon slips away.

Late Summer: Sydney
For Vivian Smith

The dripping rain brings no relief:
it deepens the darkness with sound.
As insects and frogs make their noise,
traffic replies in the distance.

I make a drink in the kitchen.
The ice cracks in the water,
musical like wind-chimes at night.
These evenings are simply dark days.

The tropical green is not given
as some consolation for heat.
The grey clouds threatened all day,
but brought no glory of thunder.

Home Beautiful

The breeze touches a yielding dress;
branches wave with no-one in mind;
the car crouches like a cat;
the road's a river turning on and off.

Inside the floors creak, white walls are silent;
clothes hang patiently for days;
the child's bed dreams of years to come;
chimneys tunnel to the sky.

Sunday Night

The disappointments of friends,
frustrations of family,
the body's sad incompetencies,
the pathos of parenthood,
love's old immensity.
As if they could all
coalesce here in this room
on a dark Sunday night
with the lamp on the chair,
the bed, the books, the
distant traffic in the wind.
What could they have to say to you?
What could they have to say?

Grief

Grief is not clean,
not a fire that
torches through undergrowth
where forgiving seeds are primed.

Grief is a flood;
and the water line will
mark the walls forever.
Walking through, you
imagine the cost,
unsure of whether
you can face the subsidence —
the muddy tools,
a lifetime leeched of colour.

Garlands

In Coniston we stand by someone's grave.
A garland of stone is laid at its head
which threads a cross for the wind to take hold.

Here are words and roses cut into stone
with real luxury, as if time was
to rehearse figures of giddying richness

in languages now almost forgotten.
How many ways are there to speak of the dead?
Stones sing out, but roses are silent.

We leave and shade our eyes from the sun.
Our hands in the air show patterns of blood;
antique houses hang across the flickering lake.

What Light Is
After Johnson

The day is still;
A clear pattern of light
Through lace is almost as
Old as blue skies.

The Dictionary
Of National Biography
Stands guard against forget-
fulness and time.

But the day is
Only held still by the
Shifting trees and shifting
Light on my desk;

And at this edge
Of the day I can hear
Shouting children after
School turn and say

'We all *know* what
Light is,' then leave without
Definition, leaving
Days like this which

Were spent watching
Through windows, and blinds bleach-
ing light on the blackboard,
   The day's lesson

   As still as the
Dictionary by my desk:
Dark and unopened,
   It answers my questions.

Autobiographical

I stand before an old window
  And see set out, like
  A painting or the arch
Of an old stage that says

'Forever': white sand merely glimpsed
  Behind the foreign trees,
  The dull cliffs covered with
Blinding houses that are closed to

The midday sun; the sky is the
  Kind of blue surrounding
  Islands; a single cloud
Sits like a flower in an empty

Room: a childhood day, perhaps. But
  This scene I have never
  Witnessed. The blue is the
Blue of my father's eyes; the trees

Have all been uplifted from far
  Away within my mind.
  I have rescued this coast
From the edge of the world, and now

I must return to the blind in
  The study, the tick of
  The clock; my life harboured
In this delicate dark night.

Metaphor

This window is
A lens; the sun turns bold,
And comes from everywhere
To leave its prints

On everything.
The window's lace is cast
In a new life upon
The wall, in and

Out of focus.
Looking out the window
I look through the stitches
And patterns of

Old taste. But on
The wall, alive, is a
Sign that seeks attention
For a moment.

Like metaphor,
The everyday is blurred,
Almost an advocate
For something that

Is lost. It seems
To say so much. Liquid
Lines upon the wall
Are memories of

Nowhere, cast by
Light and darkness. Outside
It's bright, but it is only
    Seven degrees.

The Same River

Serenity
Is the hardest God: 'Just
Give me everything and
I'm yours,' it says,

A voice you've heard
Once or twice; by the
River, perhaps, or the
Edge of a day

Which seemed to stretch
Into eternity,
When love and indifference
Bled into one.

But were they just
Moments in the story
Which has a hold on both
Sides of the old

Puzzle about
The river? Is it the
Same river? you ask your-
self as you glide

Toward the ocean,
Serene as the water:
A statue exploding
Over the stones.

The Story's End

An echo without a source;
A fine day when you are ill;
Memories of childhood sadness;

The night train which never stops;
A quiet house full of noise;
Your empty clothes in the air;

Each day a day of the week;
The story's end imagined
Day after day after day.

His Hands

[1]

LEFT HAND

The hair is flattened grass upon a wind-
Strewn beach; beneath the skin are the frozen
Waterways of a distant planet, and
On the palm the ancient markings of an
Unknown moon.

[2]

RIGHT HAND

Miniature elephant knees upon the
Bones of expression, and pale moons rising
Above each one; a thumbnail sketch of its
Entire life; it holds a pen as if it
Was a lover. Beyond it is the world.

After a Line Abandoned by Chris Wallace-Crabbe

The world is full of little animals —
   the cats with measured steps
perform their scholarly enquiries
   to chairs and doors; the legs
of squid are really lips (with thanks to time

Which frees the doodling gene 'Mutation').

Small birds trace maps like battle lines across
   the sky; and possums stare
away the blesséd emptiness of night,
   while underneath a star
you call to moths, these creeping things, and whales:

'Release the silent hamster of desire.'

Boarding School

[1]

School girls in long, dark plaid,
long past the games they played,
now walk the streets
like nuns on heat.

[2]

For Carnival nothing is turned upside down;
(there is a tent with credit card facilities):
we look up at the sky
and curse the joy-riding helicopter
which lands beside the goal-posts.

[3]

The European trees seem real enough,
though one has doubts about the architecture.

[4]

Promises and promiscuity walk
hand in hand
to the corner shop.

Part II

Domestic Elegies

'long, fleeting years'
GUY DE MAUPASSANT

WHAT TO DO WITH THE EVENINGS (I)

It's dusk and looks
like rain. Television

tells you how warm it is.
The change is on its way.

This is the time regret
softens and darkens

like a bruise,
and evening is
            long enough

for years of memory or
two or three more hours of television.

Or you could just hit the streets:
one more suburban

obsessive, taking himself
out for a walk.

God

God, the lonely father,
shuffles through the
corridors of heaven,
haunted by angels—
memories of desire,
the source of nostalgia.

He's got forever to
remember, too many
books to think
about reading, a CD
collection to get
him through the next
millennium.

He stopped checking
the phone machine years ago.
He watches television
through the endless night.
    Everything
he looks at is in
his own image.

You'd come home at night
　like a plane landing.
We'd wait for you to
　disembark from yourself,
put your hand-luggage
　on the table.

WHAT TO DO WITH THE EVENINGS (II)

Why do we
read books, watch
TV and stuff?
So as to forget,
to not think of how
things really are.
You discovered
that years ago,
when you were
a kid, but you've
read too many books,
watched too much TV
until you've almost—
but not quite—forgotten.

We are dark water,
  but shallow.
Looking up,
we might contain the sky.

Thinned out by age.
If you held me up to the light
You would see the dark
                flowers of your hands.

You decided that
  you had lived
on the surface
  of your life

for too long—
  you needed
to become an
  explorer, and so

you went down
  into yourself,
a long time ago.
  The rope is still

taut, but no
  matter how far
down I look, I
  cannot see a thing.

Their green desires
rose between them,

until one day a maze
appeared so thick

and tall neither one
of them could see or hear the other.

Succedaneum

(1)

If the message on the piece of paper
  is 'I love you',
What about the brick it's wrapped around?
And what about the window?

(II) DELIGHT

Delight, it turns out,
is a lawyer
staying back at work,
kicking off her shoes
and opening a bottle of red,
while clients' files
are safely locked
in metal cabinets,
each one annexed
by a division of the alphabet.

(III) ARGUMENT

After every
    stormy argument
there was
    the rainbow

of her smile,
    but never any gold.

(IV) OUR ARGUMENTS

Our arguments
wouldn't stand up in court.

We had to strap them
in their chairs,
hold back
their lolling heads.

Finally, after years
of meeting like this,
we looked up
and found
the judge was fast asleep.

(v)

You were always
    renewing yourself—
trying to raise
    your life into a

permanent structure.

Once I touched
    the wet paint
of your heart—
    it was sticky

and never dried.

(vi) BITCH

When we were together
it was like having shares
in Damage Incorporated.
The chairman of the board
would turn up at night,
weeping in the rain
or pointing his finger
and saying it was all
my fault.
            We'd scan
the share prices everyday
without letting the other see.
We used phrases like
'good money after bad',
until at last the whole
thing crashed. Now I'm trying
to live within my means, while
you're somewhere, dispensing
another pill from the blister
pack of your emotions.

(VII)

Once I came home
to my winking phone machine

to find an empty message—
minutes long—but not

silence, rather the ghostly
hiss of open lines:

accusatory, opaquely biographical,
confession's reverse.

(VIII) Love & Anger

How strange we
    recognize things straight
off, but not for what they
    are. You, for instance —

your quickness, your brightness:

you move fast and
    brightly through you life,
like a flame
    along a fuse.

Last Chances

(1)

She scans her torch
into his heart.

The dry grass,
the dead branches,

the bitter wind . . . the fuel.
The torch's blinding

light flashes and flares,
but can never start a fire.

(11)

It is always
    like this, or
something like this.
    I cannot love

you because I pretend I
    love someone
who does not love
    me. Meanwhile,

you have tied
    your maiden heart
to the iron railroad
    of your desire.

(III) DIURNAL

At night they
  lie side by side
in the Edenic garden
  of their bed.
They are two night-
  blooming flowers
opening under the
  moon of their bedside light.
In the morning the closed
  buds of their faces
bend over the
  the breakfast table.

(IV)

We catch our flights
And share speed's simplification.
You only move like this
When nothing lies before you.

Back home in separate houses
We shift slowly, so as not to
Catch the sharpness of tables, of chairs,
The mournful solidity of everyday life.

Part III

A Few Questions

Is it a scandal to be
expelled from the School for Scandal?

Do grand pianos put on airs and graces?

What's French for gauche?

Can anything be redeemed?

When will I be free of dreams?

Hours

Our life as clouds:
emerging as horse, as unicorn.

Massive over horizons,
we brood for hours.

Some days we perform
slow-mo arabesques, like love.

When we sleep we dream
an emptiness, vast and blue.

A Perfect Heart

(1)

Less and less of his life
was in his hands.
His hazel eyes as pale as tears.

There was nothing to be
said for all those
figures who had peopled his years:

the damaged man
                    with the perfect heart.

(11)

The heart does nothing
but stammer
its useless repetitive prayer.

(iii)

How could a thing
so melancholy, so ancient,
softer than words, smaller
than a hand, turn out
to be so mechanical,
so eighteenth century—
a messenger of nothing
but its own pathology,
waiting like a lover
for a doctor to unlock
its secrets
with his keyhole surgery?

(IV)

Only a fool
would ask where
children come from.

Do they come from the heart?

Often enough, but they inhabit
the heart, as the
wind inhabits trees.

(v)

The heart has no frontal lobes.
The heart is all fucked up.
It's a broken record.

It remembers itself every second
with a shock of recognition.
It comes to life repeatedly.

It's a blind poet, singing
O, O, O to the tired,
uncomprehending brain, who

cannot remember why or
when the heart made up
its mind not to listen to mind.

(VI)

my ironic heart
that beats with such insistence
'Perhaps . . . perhaps . . . perhaps'

The Art of Happiness
for Anthony Lynch

1. POINTILLISM

Let the spots
            before your eyes
be 1967 bright
            to form a picture of
1887 leisure —
            everything coming together:
the women in long skirts;
                        the children and fathers;
the day in its
            endless moments.

2. ABSTRACT EXPRESSIONISM

Think yourself a plain
and let your lighter self
shimmer over the dark ground

of your human memory.
Your spirit is a landscape.

3. LATE MINIMALISM

Put a window
in your ceiling
and watch the sky.

It turns out that
the colour of
happiness is blue.

Brief Lives

TS Eliot is reading Conan Doyle;
Marilyn Monroe is shaving her legs;
James Joyce is washing last night's dishes;

Elvis Presley stares with mild abstraction
Into the soothing night-light of the fridge;
Young Ned Kelly's stoking up a fire;

JFK is snoozing in the afternoon.
Someone's left the TV on and waves of
Laughter flood the cold, untenanted chairs.

Singles

Take me to the Riverina.

The wit says, 'Elvis has left the building'.

'Can you take me back where I came from?':
    Paul at 26.

1957, 1967, 1977 . . . all patterns dissolve.

Thousands of studio hours tossed to the airwaves.

Elvis Costello wore Buddy Holly glasses.

Paris 1919 or *Berlin*?

The banality of Devo.

One third of the Berlin trilogy was recorded in Switzerland.

'Get sober. Create'.

Doodoodoodoodoo doo doo doodoo doodoo.

Rock stars marry in haste and repent in leisure wear.

All work and no airplay.

Covers

for Laurie Duggan

'Long Tall Sally' in one take
by The Beatles; 'I'm Waiting
for the Man' by David Bowie
at the BBC (also 'live in
the studio'); The Flying Burrito Bros
predating the Stones' 'Wild Horses';
a camped-up glam version of
'Let's Spend the Night Together'
(Bowie again); Bryan Ferry's
early solo albums—his 'ready-mades'
showing art-school roots;
Emmylou Harris doing the
'definitive' Gram Parsons;
The Cowboy Junkies' 'Sweet
Jane'; Harry Nilsson's
'Makin' Whoopee';
Richard and Linda Thompson:
'The Dark End of the Street';
the Sex Pistols' go at 'Substitute',
strangely apposite; and later Pearl Jam's
'Baba O'Riley' also showing
rock'n'roll's intuitive love of lineage.
It's endless (but stay away
from those 'tribute albums').
In jazz, it's different.
A standard is when
the original has gone to
live quietly off the royalties.
In poetry there's parody
and homage, and then

there's translation, that strange
performance : '*I* is another'.
                              I leaf
through my old LPs,
showing them to my daughter.
She wants to do the dot-to-dot
on *Who by Numbers.* Why not?

Manifest

If I could only speak
  about the occupied
territories, about war
  and oil and the fourteen
months of lies, about
  how ASIO makes
its house calls in the
  smallest hours of the morning.
If we could speak, then,
  of how, in Ancient
Rome, a nobleman walked
  the streets with a brightly-
coloured bird that cost
  more than a slave (a
human slave); or how
  in the hour it has taken
to write this, three more
  species no longer exist
in tropical rainforests;
  or how the Americans
alone detonated over one
  thousand nuclear bombs
(which they filmed)—then
  would it be just
another of those occasions
  when one of the
honest ones turns
  to a colleague and says,
'We're all sons of bitches now'?

Mid Life

'You make your bed,
you lie about it.'
What is heroic
about finding one life

not enough? Why do we
buy so many things?
At our age this is clear:
life offers not choice, but change.

Autobiology

When your eyes are hungry
then the brain is tired.
A hand implores
and the legs are weary.
The back is strong
and the ears are blocked.
The flesh and bones
remember more than memory.

Meanwhile, the hotelier
of your heart gives you
the usual message : 'no messages'.

Rubber Bullets

The poem and death
  are always talking.
The words lie on
  the page like bullets,
like rubber bullets,
  while the most you,
dear reader, can
  hope for is tear gas.

Ghostly

For a ghost
I am strangely palpable.

I leave a hollow
in my bed when I get up.

In humid weather
my head will ache and

sometimes I have
a dodgy stomach.

I move things slowly so
nothing flies across

the room. Tiredness
makes me heavier,

as if I were on the
wrong planet. And at night

when I cross over
to sleep, I long for

my suspended body
to discover once again

the lost and spectral
insubstantiality of love,

and bring my living back to life.

One moment please

Why do we
   need so much repetition
to learn
   that nothing stays the same?

The calendar turns over
   as regular
as music, but people
   come and go,

come and go—

Distance

After all these years,
distance may make

things clearer
but not more beautiful:

all my hopeful bird life
caught in the oil-slick of your unhappiness.

The Last Summer

That summer was happiness divided by light,
though a change often came around three,

like we were children let out for the day.
The man upstairs would stake out his

four feet of balcony and immensity of sky,
drinking his way to darkness,

when he would walk down to the local
and let the genie out of the bottleshop.

Summer is for those who don't work,
and we were doing time that was running out.

What did we do with those days and nights?
Those things—hot and wet—that went without saying.

Facts of Life

So life gets factual
with its losses and reparations

and each step a border crossing.
Sometimes you wonder

how you can look so
strangely competent, and not know

the geography of the moon
or even whose face it represents;

not know the names of
plants, or even what they've

been greenly reciting
every day of your life.

The Field

Something makes the sound of an iron hinge
Long ago rusted and now beyond caring.
It may be birds or a distant wind-mill
Or a withered fence with frantic wiring,

Or a hinge which was left to itself
And now, like a bell, calls lonely things
To grind themselves upon the wind
And whittle to nothing our human songs.

Bird and Fox

I'm driving home from
   the empty campus
this Sunday dusk, creeping

down the hill that's curtly
   underscored by the
Melbourne highway

and the ruthless estate
   of houses on the
opposing hill, now hardly

a hill, an adamantine
   network of networks,
serviced or ignored by

the caravan park, the vast
   hardware shop
hangared in morose green,

two service stations, and the
   University. The blonde
transcendence of this hill

gives a sense
   of superior times.
My evergreen car cruises

past a fox,
   shaggy and red,
vividly lit

by the monstrous sun
   behind its head.
The fox indifferently

looks my way,
   then up and around
at some small violence

above it: a
   tiny bird, like indignant
thought made flesh.

I manage the speed hump,
   and make my ponderous
way to the roundabout,

leaving behind
   the hill and its
ambiguous animals,

neither picture book
   nor symbol: strange
suburban *agon*.

The naked sun, old vandal,
   sits in the rear-view mirror
and burns them out of existence.

Morning

Driving home, my daughter
now at school, the rain
falls serially, tearful
drop by tearful drop.
On the footpath is
a tarpaulin that I
mistake for a man. By the
traffic lights half way down
the hill, a slab of concrete
above a drain has quietly
collapsed, strangely discrete
evidence of an accident.
On Princes Bridge a
man walks two black dogs;
the trees overhanging the Barwon
are yellow. It could be 1966.
My car is caught in the
roundabout's gravitational pull,
then flung towards Highton.
At home in the drive way, two birds
take their morning stroll with gravity.
The car prowls into the garage.
I unlock the front door and
you are sitting exactly where
I imagine you would be.
I close the door on the morning.

Days

The calendar discreetly
  points out that our
  days are numbered.

The mountain in the distance
  writes its brutal
  contract in stone.

All the nation's hospitals
  are filled with
  ancient pictographs.

The significance of
  even these simplest of things
  still keeps evading us,

The daylight that shines through
  our house, the creatures
  that bathe in the light.

Hours

Through the potent night
we lie like larvae in sleep.
In the beds of our bodies
there are monsters called dreams.
Our brains tip themselves
slowly into spine and sheer response,
the electricity that comes and goes.
For hours the house
arches its back against the dark,
until the birds
sharpen their beaks
on the newly minted morning.

Night Fragments

These nights, we do
  improvisations of sleep—
  await the curtain call of morning.

    ∼

We bounce like stones on a lake
  from one primitive dream to another,
  until we are spent in
  the bleaching light of day.

    ∼

Our sleeping bodies: hyphens
  between two unspeakable words.

    ∼

From the toilsome field of night
  we harvest all our doings,
  and bind them to the sun.

Part IV

For Maria

Our anxieties
  like zebras in the grass;
the taste of heat
  smearing our hands;
all around, a giant
  noise that blends
into silence;
  our beautiful lust
coming down to feed.

For Maria

I had thought my body
  the shroud of my youth,
my voice a ghost
  haunting my mouth.

     ∽

I remember that look
  you gave—a thread from
a cloak of grief you
  kept to keep you warm.

     ∽

When we cut away
  those insubstantial things,
we entered into ourselves
  (textiles of eye, of lip).

'It has no edges'

for Maria Takolander

It is strong and airily thin;
it is the joyful pain within
the chest: unendurable and blesséd;
it is a word repeated, daily, as a prayer;
it is recognition's home;
it is laughter and the room
beneath the sea on which the storm is raging;
it is a look, a kiss, a touch—
those simple things that angels covet;
it is the thing within the work that fills so many days;
it is the night sky's dress in honour of our passion;
it is something understood.

Printed in the United Kingdom
by Lightning Source UK Ltd.
103897UKS00001B/138